BINGE WATCH

poems by

Kati Goldstein

Finishing Line Press
Georgetown, Kentucky

BINGE WATCH

Copyright © 2017 by Kati Goldstein
ISBN 978-1-63534-227-7 First Edition
All rights reserved under International and Pan-American Copyright Conventions.
No part of this book may be reproduced in any manner whatsoever without written permission from the publisher, except in the case of brief quotations embodied in critical articles and reviews.

ACKNOWLEDGMENTS

Reality Hands: "I AM THANKFUL FOR MY MIDNIGHT"
Inferior Planets & Voicemail Poems: "WE CAN HAVE A SECTIONAL WITH A CHAISE"
Phantom Books: "MOM," & "EITHER DID IT OR KNOWS WHO DID"
Columbia Poetry Review: "I'LL TELL PEOPLE YOU'RE MY REAL DAUGHTER"
Leviathan Magazine: "NINE DAYS," "BUTNER FEDERAL CORRECTIONAL COMPLEX INMATE 95290-004," & "THE HOUR OF LEAD"

"OMG IS THE MOON OK?!" was selected by David Trinidad and Lisa Fishman as the winner of Columbia College Chicago's 2015 Commencement Poetry Competition and appeared in the commencement program.

Publisher: Leah Maines

Editor: Christen Kincaid

Cover Art: Ben Attias

Author Photo: Alexander Glassman

Cover Design: Elizabeth Maines McCleavy

Printed in the USA on acid-free paper.
Order online: www.finishinglinepress.com
also available on amazon.com

Author inquiries and mail orders:
Finishing Line Press
P. O. Box 1626
Georgetown, Kentucky 40324
U. S. A.

Table of Contents

I AM THANKFUL FOR MY MIDNIGHT	1
NINE DAYS	2
AFTER DISCOVERING THAT MY STEPFATHER HAS BEEN PHOTOGRAPHING ME FROM OUTSIDE MY BEDROOM WINDOW	3
OMG IS THE MOON OK?!	4
TODDLERS & TIARAS	5
VARIOUS STAGES OF UNDRESS	6
LAGUNA BEACH	7
SCIENTISTS CAN'T SAVE US NOW, MOONY BOY	8
BUTNER FEDERAL CORRECTIONAL COMPLEX	9
WE'VE GOT A VIRGIN WHO SPENDS THE NIGHT IN THE FANTASY SUITE!	10
THE HOUR OF LEAD	11
EITHER DID IT OR KNOWS WHO DID	12
I'LL TELL PEOPLE YOU'RE MY REAL DAUGHTER	13
GILMORE GIRLS	14
WHEN I SAY TOTAL NON-EVENT, I MEAN A TOTAL NON-EVENT	15
FELICITY	16
BETH AM GIRL	17
NO ONE ON THE MOON IS PINK OR HELD	18
BUFFY THE VAMPIRE SLAYER	19
MOMENTS IN MY BEDROOM WHEN I THOUGHT I WAS ALONE BUT MAYBE WASN'T	20
MOM,	21
PETTY MOURNING	23
THE REAL HOUSEWIVES OF BEVERLY HILLS	24
HIGHWAYS ARE AMAZING & CRUMBLY	25
WE CAN HAVE A SECTIONAL WITH A CHAISE	26

I AM THANKFUL FOR MY MIDNIGHT

blue cardigan with the silver threads woven
in like night city windows that dot the dark—
what girls do when guys aren't around.

We could circle the earth—honey bees
assigned jobs by other honey bees. I resemble
my mother: more optimistic than biblical,

born craving sugar. She had the spots
all stitched, wishing everything would stay
built up beneath her fingernails—no forgetting

the old color of the amaryllis or shoes with soft
insides walking across a frozen lake. If x means y
& x was built in pieces, I am a giant with an

overbite; I have hundreds, hundreds of vegetables
in my fridge, necklaces in Ziploc baggies, little
plastic tigers, floor length sequin gowns, dog stories.

NINE DAYS

We packed your ties away first.
As if you had died, we folded
them and placed them in cardboard
boxes. We plucked your boxers
out the hamper, untangled them
from our bra straps; took your
razor from the shower, washed
your stubble down the drain. Still,
your scent in the vents, a can of Skoal
between the cushions of your old
recliner, a matchbook
at the bottom of the dryer.

AFTER DISCOVERING THAT MY STEPFATHER HAS BEEN PHOTOGRAPHING ME FROM OUTSIDE MY BEDROOM WINDOW

I swallow the pit of a plum,
I retch & retch
but it won't come back
up; I go to class, download
five episodes of
Buffy the Vampire Slayer
while my professor critiques
my latest short story;
I order chocolate
cake & cannoli from the pizza
place down the street; I don't feel
sad enough when one of my
classmates is killed; I think the pit
will pass or dissolve but it just
sits; I lie on my back, revise
old memories & think
I knew it.
I knew it.
I knew it.
I knew it.
I knew it.
I knew it.

OMG IS THE MOON OK?!

Such luck to believe there was a bird, so
glad to have spent my skin. This fire
is so much how it is, just too many new. I
literally copy & pasted the whole world,
just hit the future of almost. This is how
we invest in pieces, going out with a needle
& thread, the soft decay. Oh, I'm good, just
feeling less than me. Temporary, temporary.
As if there aren't already enough reasons
to get a giant rock. This is the healing of being
awake: carrots are the mad ones. I love you so
obviously. This bunch of life skin, this importance
of giving a voice to cardigans. Another day, another
beautiful raisin in the whole thing.

TODDLERS & TIARAS

SamiJo's mom Tricia works as a promoter and a Hooter's waitress to pay for pageants. Her ex-husband thinks they are a waste of money but her new boyfriend has SamiJo's logo shaved into his hair. Destiny tells her mom Sherrie that she doesn't want to do her disco dance, she wants to dance on the pole. Jennifer thinks her daughter Camarie is the total package. She named her after calamari because it's her favorite food. She likes it when Camarie wins because then she knows her kid is prettier than your kid. Tricia thinks exposing her children to whatever she can is a great way to be culturally diverse. Also, ever since Tricia's breast augmentation, SamiJo has been obsessed with bras. Tricia thinks SamiJo is more like seventeen than two. Jennifer thinks Camarie's facial beauty will carry her a long way. Unfortunately, her red dress is a little small around the stomach area. She hopes no one will notice if Camarie keeps her hands to her sides. Sherrie takes Destiny to get a spray tan. Destiny won't put down her pacifier so ends up with a pale ring around her mouth. Tricia never has to choreograph routines for SamiJo because she is so advanced, she has understandings that six and seven year olds don't have. At the *Beautiful Me Disco Diamond Pageant*, the judges look for facial beauty and sparkle on stage. The first contestant's favorite hobby is playing with bubbles. SamiJo forgets to look at the judges during the beauty-wear portion. Jennifer asks Camarie if she thinks she will do better than SamiJo. She does. The judges like the open back on Camarie's dress. Destiny forgets to blow the judges a kiss. The judges don't think today was her day. None of the girls win the "Grand Supreme" title but their moms think they definitely will next time.

VARIOUS STAGES OF UNDRESS

I
you had a new lens you wanted to try out it wasn't like you did it all the time just that once or twice you don't even remember doing it you could have done a lot worse

II
i should accept you for who you are like the men in your court mandated sex offenders group they make you look like a saint i should be grateful you aren't one of them

III
i'm so dramatic if you wanted to you would have done it

IV
you're not a real pedophile you never actually had sex with kids just watched videos of other people doing it and you prefer the ones where they look like they enjoy it

LAGUNA BEACH

The weekend before Nicole Schmidt's
bat mitzvah, I buy a dress: strapless, black
with white polka dots, Jessica McClintock.
The skirt, lined in red tulle, fans
when I spin.

SCIENTISTS CAN'T SAVE US NOW, MOONY BOY

There was once a wet sleeping bag
inside a wet tent under a wet tree.
When the bugs arrived, they climbed
inside our ears & socks until
we died a little bit. This skull top is so soft.
It would make a lovely bed.

BUTNER FEDERAL CORRECTIONAL COMPLEX
INMATE 95290-004

Did it matter when at your graduation
I got that perfect shot of you shaking
your principal's hand and later called you
my daughter and told you I was proud?
When I took you, at ten
to the pool with your friends and snapped
pictures of you in your little suits, posing
on the lifeguard stand, cocking
your little hips? Your mom framed one and hung
it in the dining room. Did it matter
when you were eight and crashed
your bike into the palm tree at the front
of the driveway, cut your leg on a fallen
dried up frond? When I lifted you,
put Neosporin on your thigh?

WE'VE GOT A VIRGIN WHO SPENDS THE NIGHT IN THE FANTASY SUITE!

And then, it's a party like no other. And then, something goes terribly wrong. 30 girls is a lot of girls, an embarrassment of riches. Are you ready to make a baby? And then, it's a shocking cocktail party that pushes the girls over the edge. There's not really a whole lot of secrets to him. And later, it's a shocking rose ceremony like no other. Honestly, I feel like this is going to be just as much work as harvest. I know deep down I'm doing this for the right reasons. Who wants to date a farmer from Arlington? Don't be nervous. Hello blondie. Hello, farmer Chris. I'm not going to say *see you inside*. Anyway, see you inside. Let me massacre this and then you can make everyone happy. I'm here to find my wife. Do you want ten more women? I wanted to tell you that you can feel safe with me now. I sell cadaver tissue. *Learn* is a strong word. What's a cat lady? I wish I was a polygamist right now. If it's a pomegranate, then God bless it. Did anybody not like that first kiss on the first night? I know a lot of girls are working through a lot of internal emotions. The room is so quiet and all I could hear are Tara's footsteps, her heels clocking up against the hardwood floor. I kept myself completely together and then drunk girls are getting roses. I thought you would never ask. I'm just a little servant. I would rather chew glass and wash it down with a bag of hair than lose to her.

THE HOUR OF LEAD

Look at her with eyes like cups; watch
as she basks in this pin drop of light, as tears
fall pretty down her cheeks like ribbons,
like they belong there.

EITHER DID IT OR KNOWS WHO DID

I am one who will
be missed. Who enjoys police reports
as much as I do? What I have to imagine
is hold a grudge down unless work
clothes. There's no evidence anyway. I knew
they knew & they knew I knew they knew.
In a way, we kiss: hit each other with some
tire irons. While you're digging to bury my body
you'll find someone else's. You skinned my
trees, drove my car into a lake. The day after
the Pizza Hut talk I am long gone. Everyone's
a suspect & no one's a suspect plus my mom.
I remember the first overhead trunk of a car. All this
went down in the parking lot since elementary school.
We need to be exactly urgent. I was abused as a series
but how many were strangled, shooken up? Until today
maybe everything happens very fast. Tomorrow
will want nothing of my nose hairs. I'm a real tear now
on the floor. The sun is a mug.
I miss my knees.

I'LL TELL PEOPLE YOU'RE MY REAL DAUGHTER

*I'll paint your name on a bomb next to
an American flag, so when they die, they'll know
who won. In war, sometimes these things are
necessary. They'll happen anyway
so we might as well watch. I like the way you look
at yourself when you put on makeup. Touch
your cheek again. It was the war, it was my childhood
that made me do it. It was a victimless crime, it would have
happened anyway. You know I never really touched you
even though you rolled your shorts at the waistband
when you were young. Your mom was so young
when we met. Your body looks just like hers
once did. She was so stunning before
the baby weight.*

GILMORE GIRLS

Dumped in a parking lot over
the phone: a feeling like hunger
only higher: in the throat,
behind the collarbone.

WHEN I SAY TOTAL NON-EVENT, I MEAN A TOTAL NON-EVENT
-Woody Allen, 1992

Look, be logical about this.
I'm 57. Isn't it illogical
that I'm going to—
at the height of a
a very bitter
acrimonious
custody fight—drive
up to Connecticut—
where nobody likes me
in the house—I'm,
I'm in a house full
of enemies, I mean Mia
was so enraged at me and
and she had gotten
all the kids to
to be angry at me—
that I'm going to
drive up there
and suddenly,
on visitation
pick this
moment in my life
to become
a child molester?
It's just, it's just
incredible.
If I wanted to be
a child molester
I had many opportunities
in the past. I could have
quietly made a-a-
a custody settlement
with Mia and done it
in the future.

FELICITY

We have dinner with his parents:
I watch his lips, flaky & Accutane pink
as they leak pizza sauce onto his basketball shorts.
Then, he fingers me in his bedroom, door
cracked, *American Idol* sounds drifting in
from the living room. Afterwards, I slip
a t-shirt from his closet into my Old Navy tote,
take Old Cutler home.

BETH AM GIRL

Jewess with no bump, tiny nostrils: a Pinecrest miracle.
She had a CHI flat iron with ceramic plates & red suede panels
& at her bat mitzvah she made out with two different boys.
There were three chocolate fountains along with seven
professional dancers who accompanied her in performing
a choreographed number to Outkast's *Roses*.
She went skiing in Utah every winter with her best friend
who got her nose fixed when she was 14 & didn't even
pretend her septum was deviated. To have a bridge smooth
like a ski jump, a tip upturned & curved ever so slightly.
To have a dermatologist, a dinner time, a Coach purse.

NO ONE ON THE MOON IS PINK OR HELD

Red glass light slides into evening like sugar on a silver
tongue. Go play a ukulele or a trumpet or dice. Go home. Can
hotel people bake babies? Is a poem the hottest yellow? How,
in houses, should I ache? Sun up, water in your frozen ice
look. Say again your kitten is like tiger toes. Years ago
lonely wives itched sideways even when they made outside laugh
like life made wishy washy marbles into purple stars. Tomorrow
was what I tasted & salted. Girls eat ice cream—yes? Right. True.
Can we also grow houses? Can anyone get folded
or take pills? Unsafe & tiny like ants on a vine, we stand
on the street & play our violins.

BUFFY THE VAMPIRE SLAYER

wears a leather trench with chunky boots
to summon ghosts in the graveyard. I watch, naked
& sweating from a basement futon, fruit fly
trap on the coffee table.

MOMENTS IN MY BEDROOM WHEN I THOUGHT I WAS ALONE BUT MAYBE WASN'T

I.
I pick shed hairs
off my body after showers,
pinch them from my
chest, roll them into nests.

II.
After a game, I tear off my
cheerleading uniform, lie bare
chest to cold tile, scratch that spot
on my neck the polyester always chafed.

III.
Before turning out the light,
I check my mirror corners, see
a glint of something
moving—maybe leaves in the wind.

MOM,

Today it was either
Brussel sprouts
or go outside
& this week's been
heavier
than last & I've been
looking at pictures
of last week
on my phone to
remember myself
lighter so I put
some Brussel sprouts
in the oven at 350
for half an hour
& grazed the metal pan
taking them out & now
my finger pad's
bubbled & puckered
like that time I made
pancakes during a sleepover
at the West Kendall house
after Lindsay Davis's
bat mitzvah & oil jumped
while I was flipping one. Also
forgot to change laundry
again—had to run it twice, still
clothes came out smelling
yellow like that spray
you used to clean
cat pee from the carpets
of the old townhouse—

not the one
where we kept the computer
on the kitchen table &
had AOL but where
streets flooded one
hurricane & ice cream trucks
came some afternoons
& we overfed our
goldfish, found it floating
dead at the top of the tank.
Now there are little
wrinkles along the lines
of my fingerprint
extending from my
blister which throbs
every time I take it
off this bag of frozen
steamy vegetables
& I miss our old cereal bowls
with the straws built in.

PETTY MOURNING

There is only this
crushed plum:
betrayal is always
so specific.

THE REAL HOUSEWIVES OF BEVERLY HILLS

Carlton goes to a candle shop & tells the cameras how she deflects negativity by putting crystals in her bra. She tells Yolanda that crystals are earth's gifts & should be cherished. Kyle & Joyce drink coffee & wonder if Carlton has been casting spells on them. Kim & Brandi get spray tans & talk about how their sweat will be brown if they work out later. Yolanda goes to her ex-husband's mansion to prepare for her daughter's graduation party. Her ex-husband doesn't like her sneakers but her current husband thinks they are cute. Yolanda tells the cameras that this is how she knows her current husband loves her for her. Yolanda's current husband & ex-husband fist bump & then hug. On her way to the party, Brandi tells a friend that her tongue is swollen because she had an allergic reaction to aspirin but it also might be a divine intervention. Brandi arrives & tells Yolanda it is probably good that her tongue is swollen because now maybe she won't say things she doesn't want to say. Carlton promises the cameras she won't start an argument tonight. Brandi tells Lisa she hasn't called because her tongue is swollen so she can't talk. Carlton doesn't want to sit next to Kyle at dinner so she sits on her husband's lap until everyone rearranges themselves. Yolanda & Brandi sit on an indoor fountain to discuss the tension between Carlton & Kyle. Kyle comes in & gives Brandi a ring to give to Carlton because it goes with the necklace she gave her as a peace offering a few episodes back. Carlton wouldn't feel right accepting a gift from Kyle so she gives the ring back to Brandi to give back to Kyle. Lisa doesn't think the ring matches the original necklace. The women talk about eating cake.

HIGHWAYS ARE AMAZING & CRUMBLY
—after Cassavetes & Catfish

Grow young again, fountain girl—
sunless & unmilked & allowed to burst.

In a dream, the bad man died & I missed him.
Shadow sick, ate only oranges that week, slept
on a California king. I'm lazy & undomestic &
guilty of bad things, maybe
even hurt.

& then we're going to cut to another angle:
This is a house where people come in, don't we agree?

WE CAN HAVE A SECTIONAL WITH A CHAISE

Here we are watching the amaryllis change colors in the living room. Here we are learning to kiss on a dirty wooden floor. Yours was the ninth tongue to enter my mouth but the first to ever taste like a tongue should: not metallic or milky, just like mine, only yours. We are equal parts young & already dead, perfect & all wrong, quartz & aquamarine: we reflect ourselves & everything else & the sky. Here we are weaving each other's scents into blankets, printing each other's body parts onto novelty t-shirts. I want to tell you: we can have a bigger garden. I want to tell you: *we can have dogs & babies & a silver staircase or we cannot. Either way.* I want to tell you: *we can make the staircase gold if you want, or platinum. We can make it out of moonstone even.* Here you are in the bathroom mirror, plucking stray hairs from my shoulders.

Kati Goldstein is a writer and educator originally from Miami, Florida. She currently lives in Chicago, Illinois where she teaches English composition and literature courses at Wilbur Wright College. In her poetry as well as her classroom, she attempts to create spaces to explore the intersection between trauma and identity. Her work often juxtaposes appropriated text from various sources of pop culture with confessional imagery, as a means of revealing tensions and parallels between our private and increasingly public selves.

Kati received her BA in English with a concentration in creative writing from Colorado College and her MFA in poetry from Columbia College Chicago, where she studied as a Jack Kent Cooke Graduate Arts Scholar. In 2015, she read at the Poetry Foundation alongside David Trinidad as part of the Open Door Readings Series. She has received numerous awards, including first prize in the Columbia College Commencement Poetry Contest in 2015 and the Evelyn Bridges Poetry Contest in 2013. Her work has appeared in *Voicemail Poems, Reality Hands, Inferior Planets, Phantom Books, Columbia Poetry Review*, and *Leviathan Magazine* among other publications.

www.ingramcontent.com/pod-product-compliance
Lightning Source LLC
LaVergne TN
LVHW041518070426
835507LV00012B/1672